BOUNDARY DISPUTES

BOUNDARY DISPUTES
and how to
resolve them

JOHN ANSTEY
BA FRICS FCIArb

SECOND EDITION

RICS BOOKS

Published on behalf of
The Royal Institution of Chartered Surveyors
by RICS Books
Surveyor Court,
Westwood Business Park,
Coventry, CV4 8JE
UK

First edition October 1990

ISBN 0 85406 858 9

Reprinted 2001

Illustrations by Michael Cromar

Typeset by Columns Design Ltd., Reading
Printed in Great Britain by Beshara Press, Tewkesbury

Contents

Introduction

Most boundary disputes take place in suburban back gardens. Most could be avoided. Most are quite simple for two surveyors to solve. Most clients refuse to accept what their surveyors tell them.

If you think that the sweeping generalisations above are untrue, then you've never had a typical boundary dispute to settle. When it comes to back gardens – or front gardens for that matter – the old Scottish proverb 'Mony a mickle maks a muckle' may be rendered as 'Every mickle maks a muckle.'

I do not claim to be the world's leading boundary expert. From most writers this disclaimer would come as a surprise and as no surprise – very few people would have the arrogance to make such an assertion, but I did so in my two previous books in this series. However, I do feel that although there are excellent books to be found on the law of boundaries – Trevor Aldridge's *Boundaries, Walls and Fences*, published by Oyez Publications, and *Boundaries and Fences*, written by V. Powell Smith and published by Butterworths, are obvious examples – there is no practical handbook for the layman or the not very experienced surveyor. I have dealt with a number of interesting and difficult boundary disputes, and I hope that I can offer some tips on how to solve at least the straightforward problems.

Of course, I shall deal with the law, but in fairly simple terms. The main idea of this slim volume is to point out the obvious, and one or two less obvious, ways of finding out where a boundary is or was.

If you are land agent to Lord Desai, and you are anxious for help in sorting out the boundary with the Earl of Gell's estate in Scotland, I do not recommend you to buy this book. I might just possibly have some intelligent advice to offer if I were presented with such a problem on the ground, but I have no helpful generalities to offer in theory. All the boundary disputes with which I have been concerned have been either in domestic gardens or between

1

commercial buildings, and they have nearly all been over a few inches.

Much of what I have to say now seems blindingly obvious to me, and I expect it will to any experienced surveyor, so I don't think that I can recommend him to buy this book, either. However, when I was groping my way towards knowledge, while appearing – I hope – to my clients to be in complete command of the situation, I would have been very glad to have had some obvious things pointed out to me. I can therefore safely recommend the young me – or my near equivalent, since a replica is too much to hope for – to buy this guide.

Finally, let me commend this book to the layman. My workload these days is such that, if I can give advice down the telephone which saves a potential client from wasting several hundred pounds in employing me to come and tell him that he has no case, I am delighted to do so. If buying one of my books will help to save the client from similar expenditure, I am delighted. I venture to think that many costly disputes would be avoided if only the parties could look rationally at the disputed area. Purchase of this book is the first rational act, and may I hope that the same calm good sense will prevail until the matter is resolved.

Chapter 1

Deed plans and their uses

Do you know where your deed plans are? Do you know what they look like? I do. Why? Because I recently had a disagreement with the local highway authority over the curtilage of my house. And that's when most people first start looking to see exactly what they own. They get on well with their neighbours, and when the fence falls down no one worries very much: it makes it easier to borrow the lawn mower or lend the roller. But then the neighbours retire to the country and the new owners want a proper fence, so they have a new one put up – in the wrong place. At least, that's the opinion of the long-term residents, and that's when such disputes normally start.

The first question to ask is: whose duty is it, if anyone's, to maintain a fence on that side of the garden? You can find this out by referring to your deeds. There may be some words that will help, and there will probably be a plan. First, find the deeds.

I suppose that 95%, or perhaps even more, of the property deeds in Britain are physically held by the mortgagees. Because I was doing a job for the Halifax Building Society I was privileged, during a visit to their head office, to see where they stored the deeds of all their borrowers. I forget all the statistics, but I think that it ran to over three miles of shelving in three storeys of basement, with a wonderful automated system of file retrieval. (If the power failed, experienced mountaineers were needed.) It is unlikely that you had the foresight to keep a copy of the deeds when you bought the house – if you did, I congratulate you – so you must set the automated wheels in motion, or whatever system your source of finance uses, and obtain a copy.

You are looking for words saying something like: 'the fence on the eastern boundary is to be maintained by the owner of (your property)'; or 'all walls and fences are party walls and fences, jointly maintainable'. If there are no such helpful clauses – or even if there

3

are, and you cannot tell east from butter – look at the plan. This
may have one or more 'T' marks on it (Fig. 1).

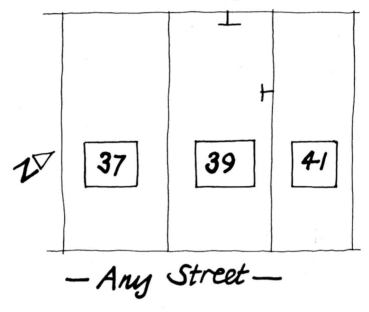

Fig. 1.

The 'T' indicates that ownership of a boundary feature lies
with the owner within whose land it appears. Therefore, in my illustration, number 39 owns the fence on his right (as he looks out of
his back window) and the one at the bottom of his garden. You can
see why 'the eastern boundary' may not be immediately obvious. If
there is a duty to maintain those features, which will not be apparent without reading the deeds, the 'T' marks will make it clear
where that duty lies.

According to a kindly gentleman, employed by the publisher
to make sure that there are no stupid mistakes in my manuscript – I
hope he's done his job well – the most frequent source of dispute
about boundary feature ownerships is the attachment of objects
such as trellises or washing lines to 'my wall'. Technically, if you own
the wall or the fence, you are within your rights in objecting to such
affixing. He says (the kindly gentleman) that the London County
Council used to collect licence fees for allowing people to attach
things to their (the LCC's) walls.

4

If – to go back to the situation I postulated a few paragraphs ago – your neighbour is carefully erecting a fence for which you are legally responsible, there are a number of options open to you. If you're happy with its appearance and position you can, like Brer Fox, lie low and say nothing. If you're on friendly terms, you may wish to offer to contribute to – or even to bear – the cost. If you're confident that the fence is not on your land, and you do not like the look of it, you could put up your own version, face-to-face with your neighbour's, thus fulfilling your legal obligation and giving yourself what you want to look at. At least you will know what your legal position is.

It's quite possible that your neighbour, having newly purchased his house, and having observed the dilapidated fence when viewing the property, is well aware whose duty it is to keep the fence up, and he may ask you politely to do so. Equally politely, you should check that he has got his facts right – it is not unknown for the contrary to be the case – and, if he has, comply. According to Mr Aldridge (op. cit.), however, it is very difficult to pass on a binding covenant to maintain a fence on freehold property, so that if you are prepared to fall out with your neighbours, you could always challenge them to make you comply. You should be warned, however, that the Court of Appeal has held (in *Egerton* v. *Harding*, 1975) that it is possible for a fencing easement to be acquired, so you might be on a loser.

If you are a freeholder on a newly developed estate, or a lease-hold owner, it is much more likely that you will be bound. However, (contrary to what many people think) surprisingly often there is no obligation to maintain a fence or wall at all. You may own it, but you do not necessarily have to strive officiously to keep it alive. Nor, con-trariwise, may your neighbour have any duty to succour it. Once again, I would urge you to be sure of your ground before you start either antagonising the people you have to live next to, or lining the pockets of solicitors and surveyors with your hard earned money. Mostly, they don't need it.

Never trust dimensions on a deed plan. You may think that that is an extraordinary thing to say. Surely if the length and breadth of your garden are clearly marked, that's all you need, isn't it? Oh, that it were so. Let me relate two recent cases of mine.

In the first, a friend of mine (by the way, never work for friends, except the very closest, and even then only if you're abso-lutely sure of their friendship: one of the very few whom I would put in that category absolutely refuses to work for the subject of this anecdote, who is also a friend of his) had a fence fall down between his garden and that of his neighbour. It was allowed to stay down too long, so that memory and record of its exact position both faded. When the time came to re-erect it, there was no agreement as to where it should go, so both parties got out their deed plans.

My friend's plan showed that his garden was eighteen feet wide at the bottom; next door's plan indicated a width of twenty-two feet for his plot. Unfortunately, between the fairly rigid fences on the opposite side of the respective gardens, there was only a distance of thirty-eight feet to play with. The more numerate among my readers will instantly realise that this left us two feet short. The very numerate will appreciate that this amounts to about 5% of the whole.

When one is dealing with such narrow back gardens, two feet is a lot of width. At least one and probably both parties were going to be very unhappy. Eventually (see the maxim about working for friends, above) I bowed out, so I don't know how it was settled, but it shows the degree of reliability attached to plans (Fig. 2).

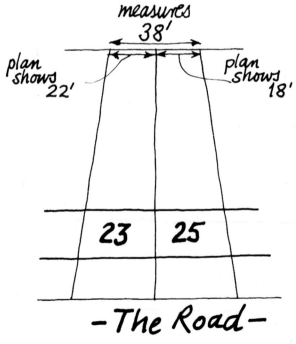

Fig. 2.

The second case is heading for a five-day court hearing, but the difficulty in this one is that a figured dimension of 287 feet (or some such figure) was given against a wavy line. How can you be sure what the waves and kinks are, unless each one is separately dimensioned – and angles shown as well, preferably? I have refused even to try to measure the boundary in question, but I think that the other side may rely heavily on it (Fig. 3).

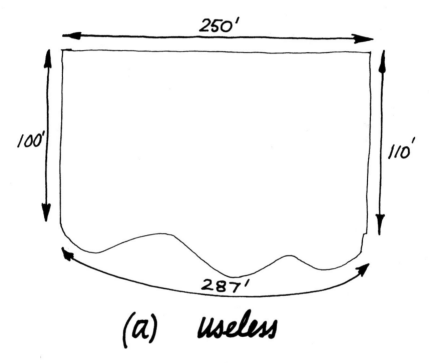

Fig. 3.

It is of no relevance to this point, but worth noting in general, that no one is quite sure of the status of the plan, or who put the figures on it. Nor was the status of the plans certain in the first case I have described. Always check your documents for authenticity, and look to see that no unauthorised additions have been made.

Writing this paragraph after the hearing of the case illustrated above, I can now tell you that the other side used the most up-to-date surveying apparatus, accurate to fractions of a second, to try to justify this vague plan. I should have been hopelessly at sea if I had tried to match them at their own game, since the last time I surveyed a comparable area we were using a Gunter's chain, and when I spent a day on practical surveying with the College of Estate Management, the resolution of my survey figures proved me to be standing on a six foot high post – very useful, when you're my size, but not, unfortunately, true.

If the original plan had been like the illustration below, then their high-tech wizardry would not only have baffled me, but would also have been useful. Just as, however, you need a place to stand in order to lever the world aside, as Archimedes pointed out, you can't make a silk survey out of a sow's plan.

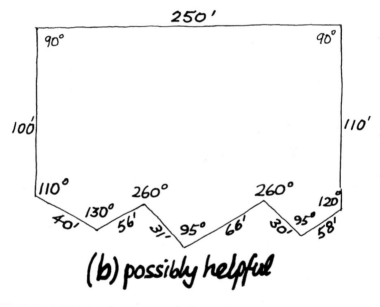

Fig. 4.

Indeed, even if you are dealing with what looks like a rectangular plot, and all four dimensions are given, you still can't be absolutely sure that you know where everything should be. If the angles are not right – 90°, I mean – then you could have a rhomboid plot. Alternatively, you could have a rhomboid plan and a right-angled

8

plot. It all depends on whether the draughtsman or the site agent was better at angles.

Sometimes only the original deed plan will tell the whole truth, so that even the best available copies don't reveal all. The next anecdote will illustrate this.

A client owned a house in north London. He purchased the site next door, on which the pair of his semi-detached house had stood, but had been demolished, and later he resold it, retaining his original house. An argument then arose about the ownership of what had – at least at one time – been the wall between the houses. My client was certain that when he sold the vacant plot he had retained the whole wall. The other side were equally sure that they had the right to use it as a party wall for their new building.

All the plans produced by my client, copied from the deeds and, as far as I could tell, undoctored, seemed to indicate that he was right, but a photocopy is only a photocopy and I decided that I ought to inspect the original title in the Land Registry. I knew lesson number one, that you had to be in possession of a valid authority from the owner to inspect his title (the law has since changed, allowing the inspection of other people's titles), but I did not know lesson number two: always make an appointment in advance, to allow time for the title to be retrieved from whatever system the Land Registry uses. It therefore took two trips to Harrow in order to see the document.

When the pie was opened, the bird that began to sing was not serenading my client. The red line clearly ran through the middle of the wall. Even now that I knew the truth, and with the original in front of me, when I looked at the photocopies I still couldn't be sure where the line was.

Shakespeare said that (and I believe I have quoted it else-where) 'crooked figure may attest in little place a million'. The thin red line on a deed plan is always several inches thick, and can be a foot or so. Scaling off a deed plan which does not bear dimensions is an even more inaccurate way of proceeding than relying on the figures – and I hope that I've shown how reliable that is. Deed plans have their uses, but they also have their limitations. You should certainly not embark on a boundary dispute without seeing what your plans can tell you, but you shouldn't pursue an acrimonious and expensive argument based solely on their evidence.

Chapter 2

Land Certificates and housing land

As I remarked in the chapter on deed plans, even apparently authoritative documents can be distinctly lacking in accuracy. Not only that, but if they are by any remote chance accurate, they are on so small a scale, certainly when they are to a typical Land Certificate scale of 1:1056 or 1:1250, that any attempt to obtain reliable dimensions from them is doomed to failure. On a recent case in Epsom, I was horrified to hear that a chartered surveyor of many years' experience was hoping to support a claim of inches by scaling off a title plan, and whereas on a deed plan a line may be as much as a foot thick, on a Land Certificate plan it can hardly fail to be at least a foot thick. After all, at 1:1250 a line which is one-hundredth of an inch thick represents about a foot in real life. And one-hundredth of an inch is not a very thick line. A plan that I consulted against which to check this line of argument, had some lines on it which were certainly thicker than one thirty-second of an inch, which is the equivalent of about three feet. Trying to scale accurately from undimensioned plans like this is therefore just a waste of time. Don't do it.

You may think that I am going on rather a lot about this, but it seems to need saying. You'd be surprised what accuracy people are inclined to expect of their Land Certificates, and they seem capable of believing whatever they measure from them, even when the facts on the ground make it perfectly obvious that the measurements can't be trusted. One of the worst causes of offence in this connection is the housing estate. By that, I do not necessarily mean the massive Greater London Council (or other local authority) development – although I did have at least one case which sprang from slovenly conveyancing on just such an estate. I mean, in fact, any grouping of several houses which are all laid out, and perhaps also built, by one developer.

What frequently happens is that someone in the developer's office draws a neat, regular plan, on which all the plots are beautifully drawn, with right-angled corners, and equal-sized frontages.

11

The plan is then taken to the site where someone else, with less enthusiasm for precision, lays it out on the ground. If you're really lucky, he uses a very simple device for the angles, and a metal tape for the measurements. If not, he sets out the corners by eye and uses a cloth tape. Or he guesses the lot.

Whatever the standards of accuracy aimed at, the achievement often falls short of the aim, and you may be left with the last plot over- or under-sized. Or the middle plot. Or both ends. Very rarely is the poor, harassed site agent (or whoever) going to go back and take six inches off here and there, in order that the skimpy plot he's found himself stuck with should retrieve its missing three feet or so.

This wouldn't matter, of course, if the purchaser were simply buying what he saw on the ground. In truth, he is, but when the conveyancer is using the original layout plan, and so sells the house-buyer a plot which is three feet wider on paper, there is going to be trouble sooner or later. (There is some comfort to be had from the recent case in Chiswick, where the Judge held that the purchaser had seen half an acre and bought half an acre, even if the particulars had described it as three-quarters.) If both parties' solicitors checked that the plan measurements matched the site ones, there would be some hope of agreement and accuracy, but that very rarely happens, and the Land Registry will probably accept the nice, neat series of plans with which the developer will provide them.

Then along comes another gale unheralded by the Met Office, and the fence blows down. Where to put it back? 'Well, the site plan says our garden is thirty feet wide' – and then the trouble begins. I shall have a lot more to say about this later, but the lesson for now is: don't expect the plans necessarily to match the plot; and if you're the first purchaser, do any quibbling before you sign on the dotted line, rather than after. At this stage there is some hope of getting any deficiencies in the plot made good. If you're a subsequent purchaser, your chances of shifting boundaries, to which your neighbours will by now have become quite attached, are not very high.

Chapter 3

Words or pictures?

One picture is worth a thousand words – except, unfortunately, when one is dealing with legal matters. If the words of a deed contradict something shown on a plan attached to it, the words prevail. The plan only governs if the deed specifically so states. It is very important, therefore, to be sure what your starting point is when you set out to decide where a boundary should be.

Don't just unquestioningly accept a plan which your client gives you. Ask to see the deed it belongs to, if there is one. If it doesn't come with a deed, where does it spring from? Does anyone on the other side accept it as a true record, so that any argument is only about interpretation, or is the provenance of the plan itself in dispute?

As I am not really setting out to guide you on how to avoid boundary disputes, but only on how to settle them once they have arisen, this is not the place to lecture you on the proper form of words to use in a deed to make sure that your plan has the right status. Nor should I now tell you how to draw an accurate plan – which is just as well, since I'm not very good at it. I advise you, however, to make sure that you are provided with a good plan, and a good solicitor to incorporate it into the deeds, if that is one of the matters you have to deal with.

Landlord and tenant plans are notorious for their inaccuracy. I once occupied part of a second floor, the whole of which had been let to me, if you believed the colouring on the plan. Fortunately there is rarely much doubt about who actually holds what, and while there might be a legal dispute as to the validity of a lease, there is not really likely to be a dispute about whether the boundary runs through the second or third desk from the right, nor even which office is really meant to be included. I knew perfectly well that my friend Tom held the rest of the second floor – which is why we're still friends over twenty years later. (It's also why, incidentally, when a lad straight from school came to me for a job, armed with a reference from Tom, who had no idea that his young neighbour was applying to me, I offered him employment straight away. This anecdote has absolutely no relevance, except that the young man later left to complete his training elsewhere, after five years with me and has now rejoined me as a partner.)

Faced with unreliable lease plans, you are more likely to have arguments about measuring what is demised: at skirting level or shoulder level; including or excluding the covings; and whether some spaces are common parts or lettable areas. But that's for another book.

Chapter 4

Fixed and general boundaries

When land is registered, and the Register records that the boundaries have been fixed, then so far as they can be traced and identified you can be confident in the exact position of them. If anyone else ever proved that they were in the wrong position, you could bring an action against the Land Registry who have, by their indication that the boundaries are 'fixed', given you an indemnity against any variation. Unfortunately, having your boundaries formally fixed is even more expensive than having the same thing done to your teeth. Every neighbour has to be notified, all the various roots of the title produced, and a survey made of the land in question, to a high degree of accuracy. Sometimes even the Land Registry gets things wrong. In a recent case in Cheltenham, my client had bought first from a larger plot, so that no more than what was left could be conveyed to the second purchaser. This latter then registered what he claimed to own, and fenced it. My client objected to the line of fencing, and I agreed that he had been deprived of some of his land. To my surprise it was not his surveyor I met to thrash out the dispute, but someone from the Land Registry. They, having wrongly registered some of my client's land to another, now had to pay all the costs of putting it right, including my fees and the bill for moving the fencing. (I got to visit the magnificent Arts and Crafts furniture display in the Cheltenham Museum: no charge.)

Usually, unless the boundaries have been fixed, the plan filed at the Land Registry will only indicate general boundaries. Being based on the Ordnance Survey, it shows the position of physical features but cannot attempt from that base to indicate ownership. Incidentally, I was about to write that you could rely on the accuracy of the features shown on the OS, but now that this once splendid organisation is avowedly trying to get away from the notion that it is there as a public service, and is more interested in the promotion of 'map products', that happy state of affairs may not be true for very much longer. Land surveyors in private practice can comfort themselves with the thought that, if standards decline at the OS, it should produce more work for the private sector.

If you want the position of one particular boundary settled, or the ownership of a certain feature, you can ask the courts for a declaration as to its true position. Since any dispute about the fixing of registered land is likely to end up in the same court, it's probably just as easy to go to the court in the first place if you expect any arguments with your neighbours as to the identity of the boundary. Mr Powell Smith (op. cit.) will give you more detail on the legal aspects of this point.

I cannot stress too often how much cheaper it is – not to mention making for better relations while you continue to live next to each other – to approach your neighbour in a spirit of friendly co-operation in jointly determining any point where there may be doubt. To say: 'Since the fence fell down, I can't really tell where the boundary is. Can you remember where it ought to be?' is much more likely to produce an amicable settlement than if you simply put it back up where you think it ought to be, even if you get it right. Believe you me, it's well worth giving up an inch or two of garden in most cases, and much, much less expensive than fighting about it, especially in court.

This is general advice on personal relations, rather than boundary disputes, but do try to see your neighbour face-to-face if you want to discuss anything, rather than just write to him. Unfortunately, even that is not an infallible method of settling disputes: I've had a number of clients say to me that they took the plans in next door, or invited their neighbours in for a cup of coffee, and everything seemed friendly and agreed, but as soon as the workmen started to put the fence up (or whatever) the neighbour went berserk and called the police. Sometimes both sides tell much the same story and allege all sorts of villainy by the other, such as deliberately sprinkling weed killer across the boundary on to the rose bed. Human nature is very difficult. You can but try.

Chapter 5

Adverse possession

Strange as it may seem to those who don't know these things, you can acquire someone else's land simply by taking very solid possession of it. If, therefore, one of these walls or fences, the correct position of which we are making such a fuss about in this book, has been in the 'wrong' place for twelve years, that can become the 'right' place.

There are, of course, certain requirements which have to be pretty firmly satisfied before you will be recognised as the owner of the land you have stolen. If you ever acknowledge to the rightful owner that you are squatting, time would start to run again from the date of that acknowledgement. What's more, your occupation and use of the land must be in such a manner as obviously to enjoy it for your own purposes, and to debar the rightful owner from his intended use.

It's virtually essential that you should enclose any land you are claiming, with a sound wall or fence. Simply to cultivate the land would be very unlikely to be enough. Indeed, in a recent case (*Dear v. Woods*, 1984) – very curiously decided, as far as I could tell from the reports – asphalting part of a front drive and even fencing it was held not to be enough to exclude next door from ownership of the disputed area.

It's harder still to get adverse possession against the Crown: there it takes thirty years. There are other cases, too, where the time will be extended, such as when the owner was under a legal disability when the right of action first arose – and time runs out after thirty years even in those deserving cases.

Of course, deliberately to encroach upon someone else's land, fence it off, and use it as your own is theft, so I am not encouraging you to try to prove adverse possession against the rightful owner. You have to know the legal position, however, in order to protect your own land against adverse possession by an acquisitive neighbour

– and also to know when it is probably not worth attempting to reclaim what was once yours.

I've often wondered about those back gardens which abut railway lines. At one time I used to commute from a station from the platforms of which you could see a number of plots being cultivated, and even enclosed, between the original rear fences of the houses and the railway embankment. Some owners had even knocked down their rear fences entirely. I think it probable that they were not excluding the railway's use of the land.

As this edition goes to press, there is a faint possibility that the time for adverse possession may be extended to twenty years, instead of twelve. It is, after all, rather curious that you can acquire land more quickly than you can obtain a right over it. However, the possibility is very faint indeed – but keep your eyes open.

Chapter 6
How large is too little?

De minimis non curat lex. The law does not concern itself with trifles. How large, therefore, does the disputed area of land have to be before the courts will be prepared to order rectification of a boundary? This question is very similar to that which is asked in *Rights of Light and how to deal with them* (see the third edition of the excellent book on that subject published by RICS Books, 1998), as to what is meant by small. The best legal opinion obtained on that – and I fancy that it might apply equally well here – is that it would not be large.

It is always very difficult to get the courts to lay down hard and fast rules – which are easier for practitioners to use in advising clients, and ever so much easier for lay people to understand. If you were able to say (if you were the adviser) to your client, 'The courts have held that to move a suburban back garden boundary two inches is *de minimis*, but to move it three inches is actionable', life would be straightforward. However, even when we had a nice simple rule to follow in rights of light cases (the 50/50 rule, which said that if 50% of a room remained well lit it hadn't been injured) the courts soon returned us to a state of indecision by saying that it wasn't to be relied on for certain. Very jealous of their prerogatives, are the courts.

One of my favourite anecdotes concerns the case in which I was instructed by a black man, who alleged that his neighbour used to sing 'Ol' Man River' loudly in his garden, to annoy him. The white man next door complained that his neighbour (one of the quietest men I ever met) used to hold noisy parties all the time. When my client renewed the fence between their respective back gardens there was bound to be trouble.

I was instructed through solicitors (who, as a matter of interest, later disappeared without seeing that I was paid) and carefully surveyed the scene of the crime. I produced a plan (Fig. 5) which showed that the greatest distance which the fence had strayed from the straight and narrow (the back gardens were approximately

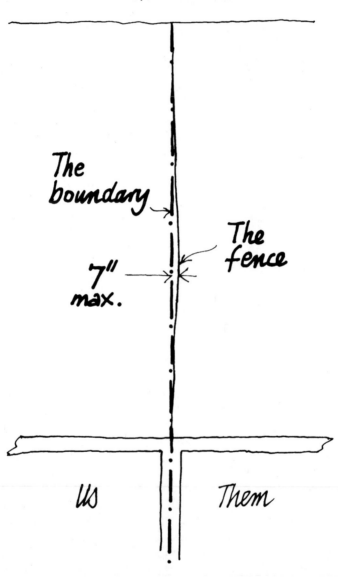

Fig. 5.

thirty feet wide) was seven inches. 'Marvellous,' said the (still present at that time) solicitors. 'That's *de minimis*.'

The other side's expert gave his evidence; I gave my evidence; the judge gave his decision: 'I accept Mr Anstey's evidence entirely, and find for the other side.' In his opinion, seven inches was not *de minimis* in suburban back gardens.

You may be aware – especially if you've read other works by the same author – that the courts are extremely reluctant to lay down rigidly fixed guidelines. This decision does not, therefore, give you licence to assert that a tapering movement of seven inches, or the wrongful enclosure of about eight square feet, will always be actionable. Still less does it allow you to assert that any smaller change would not be corrected by the courts. It is a question of fact and degree in each case, but at least this decision gives you a useful pointer.

The best help I can give you in the opposite direction comes from a case which involved a party wall – or not, as the boundary might be. If the wall was astride the boundary, then it was a party wall under the London Building Acts, and those who were seeking to raise on it would have to serve notice. If it was wholly on their land, they could do what they liked. There was no suggestion that it might be wholly on my client's side of the boundary.

The strong point in favour of the other side was that the wall and their building appeared to have been built at the same time in the same bricks. A point in our favour was that the history of the two sites strongly indicated that they weren't, in fact, built contemporaneously. There were one or two well-fixed points lying about, and some pretty exactly stated measurements in sale particulars, conveyances, and the like. You have read of my distrust of measurements, but nonetheless I started from one of the best fixed points and measured to the wall. If the measurements on the plans were accurate, the nine inch wall was 1.5 inches on one side and 7.5 inches on the other side of the boundary. (This would be quite enough to make it a party wall by definition.) I don't remember my evidence being seriously challenged on facts or disturbed in cross-examination, but the judge found that 'None of the measurements was exact enough to be relied upon for the position of the boundary', and therefore relied on the visual evidence of the consanguinity as proof that the wall belonged to the owners of the building.

This case is a hint – no more – that 1.5 inches is *de minimis*. I learn from Mr Aldridge (op. cit.) that the court will not usually entertain an action for a declaration if the subject-matter is worth less than £10. Since that stems from an 1885 case, I would have thought that, even under a government so little inclined to the indexing of pensions or pay, the courts might well fix on a higher figure today.

But for goodness sake. When you consider how accurate your measurements are likely to be, however sophisticated your equipment (and this isn't a book about advanced surveying techniques, because you rarely have a starting point reliable enough to justify their use in the sort of situations I'm describing) two inches or so are just not worth worrying about.

If there is any question of the matter falling under this head, there are even more grounds than usual for ramming down the unwilling client's throat the desirability of forgetting about the whole thing, or else reaching a settlement with his neighbour, however much he detests him. And whether or not he poisoned the roses.

Chapter 7

Party walls and 'party' walls

Between walls inside and outside London there used to be a great gulf fixed. Contrary to the views of one critic, I am aware that walls exist outside London, but as I was writing the book then under review specifically about those inside I did not say a great deal about the other kind.

Party walls inside London used to be governed by the London Building Acts, especially the Amendment Act of 1939, while everywhere else in England and Wales (Scotland is always different) common law ruled. In 1996, a public spirited group of surveyors succeeded in getting the Party Wall etc. Act through Parliament, which came into full force in September 1997, so now those two countries share the benefits which were formerly those of London alone. This grants extraordinary powers to an owner of one half of a wall to treat the other half of it almost as if it were his own. On the other hand, he cannot treat his half as if it were his own, without taking his neighbour into his confidence and, in effect, discussing with him how it should be dealt with. I could go on at length, which would help to pad out this short book, but as I have already done so elsewhere, I will simply refer you to *Party Walls and what to do with them* (RICS Books, 4th edition, 1996).

Party Structures which previously existed in the rest of the country were cut in half by the Law of Property Act 1925. I have always had a mental picture of a little man with a saw going round the country physically cutting through the middle of the wall, but the severance was, in fact, a legal one. Each party thereafter has the necessary easements of support and user in the other half, but the rights didn't go anything like as far as they did in the metropolis.

Before the 1996 Act, your rights in your neighbour's half of the wall were virtually nil. You could look to him to keep your half up, but you certainly couldn't touch his half without his express permission, unless you had by the normal – if that is the right word – legal process acquired a specific easement to do so. On the other hand, you could do what you liked with your half (though see above about support) without seeking his approval and without paying his surveyor's extortionate fees for a party wall award. The importance of this chapter to this book is that in dealing with party walls in England and Wales, precise boundaries are not always relevant to what you can or cannot do to a wall. In Scotland – and Northern Ireland for the time being – they probably still are.

In the first edition of this book, I made an elegant joke about the right to go on to a neighbour's land being comparable to the snakes in Ireland. This is no longer true, though it might as well be for all the use that the Access to Neighbouring Land Act 1992 is in providing the help that it was meant to. (For a full explanation of this Act, see the CPD study pack of the same name published by the College of Estate Management, or the Owlion tape on the subject.) Unfortunately, its operation depends on the courts (unlike the Party Wall etc. Act which is managed by surveyors) and is so unwieldy that the words 'sledgehammer' and 'nut' spring to mind. The only two cases I know of resulted in travesties of justice.

Briefly, the Act says that if you have asked permission to go on to your neighbour's land, and have been refused, you may seek consent from the courts. Access will only be granted for maintenance or repair, not new building, and may be subject to strict conditions as to time and other matters. In addition, in non-domestic cases you will have to pay handsomely for the privilege. Apart from the use of this Act, there is a rather tenuous right to go on to your neighbour's property to restore support to your own, if the neighbour is allowing it to decay.

The correct position of a boundary is therefore of considerable importance, and whereas a few feet or even yards may not matter on a moor, a few inches can be of critical importance between suburban houses. In fact, I think that resolving disputes on such issues is probably one of the most expensive ways of passing the time that can be found.

The most common cause of disputes about the position of the boundary in a party wall is eccentricity – not on the part of the owners, although there's quite enough of that flying about, but in the walls. If the wall is symmetrical then, as I say in the chapter on garden walls, you can fairly safely assume that the boundary runs down the middle. The trouble comes when the wall is shaped like the one in my illustration (Fig. 6).

The question then arises: was it built like this, astride the

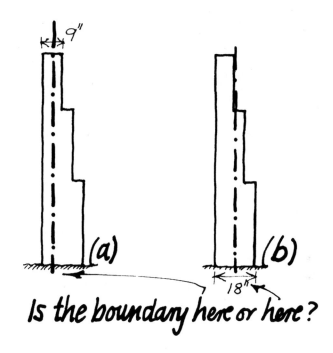

Is the boundary here or here?

Fig. 6.

boundary, or was it built as a straightforward nine inch (say) wall, which one owner has since thickened for his own purposes? The answer may depend on which parts of the wall are older, if you can tell. Look at the next illustration (Fig. 7).

If the original wall appears to be as shown in Fig. 7(a), nine inches from top to bottom, with thicknessing added by one owner on one side, presumably in order to take his new, heavier structure, you can be fairly sure that the boundary is as shown in Fig. 6(a), i.e. in the centre of the nine-inch chunk. If, on the other hand, the wall seems originally to have been lower, perhaps only two storeys high, and one owner has raised it, getting the maximum area for his new upper floors by setting his raised portion as far over as possible, as shown in Fig. 7(b), then the boundary will be as shown in Fig. 6(b), in the centre of the original eighteen-inch structure.

Now that the Party Wall Act rules, it is also important to know whether the wall has been thickened or whether it is two separate

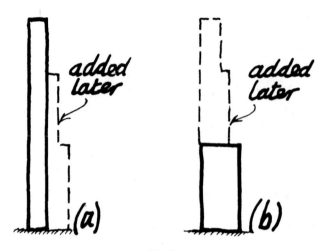

Fig. 7.

skins. If the former, then the whole wall may be a party wall, albeit eccentrically astride the boundary; if the latter, it is quite probable that each party owns one skin, and the boundary runs between them.

If you can't tell what the history of the wall is, and you are forced to guess, I would be inclined to plump for Fig. 6(a) – but that assumes that there is nothing to point you towards another or a better-founded answer. Always prefer evidence to guesses.

Chapter 8

The boundary between attached houses

An attached house can either be part of a terrace (Fig. 8) or one of a pair of semi-detached properties (Fig. 9). In this context, its most important feature is that it shares at least one wall with a neighbour.

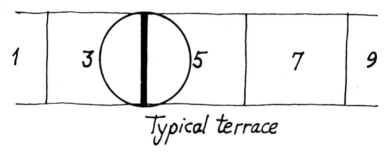

Typical terrace

Fig. 8.

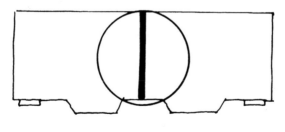

Typical pair of semi d's.

Fig. 9.

In the absence of clear proof to the contrary, such as an unequivocal statement in a deed, or a plan in which the boundary is distinctly shown to include the whole of the wall within one party's ownership, as in Fig. 10, the dividing line between the properties can be assumed to be the centre line of the common (or 'party') wall as shown in Fig. 11.

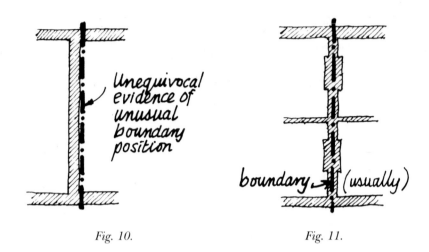

Fig. 10.   Fig. 11.

Sometimes, perhaps even usually, this sort of boundary causes absolutely no problem at all. The wall is quite straightforward, as shown in Fig. 11, and each party's ownership of, and rights in, their own half are clear.

Complications can exist, even in this simple form of dividing wall, but they tend to be complications more of use than of ownership. One such is when the builder has skimped on the brickwork and has either intermingled the flues, or at least only just kept them on their own side of the boundary (Figs. 12 and 13).

Fortunately, the sort of flue illustrated in Fig. 13 is comparatively rare. When it occurs, however, it has been known to cause confusion as to the position of the boundary. The chap who is doing some work to the chimney breast in his property opens up the flues, and concludes that his ownership must extend at least as far as the back of the flues, and possibly half a brick beyond it. I don't think that it does. I know of no leading case on the subject, but I would suggest that each party has an easement to have his

28

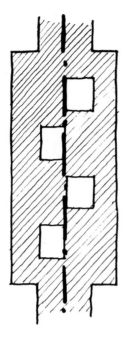

Fig. 12.

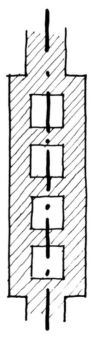

Fig. 13.

29

smoke or fumes pass up the flue within his neighbour's property and, should he choose to rebuild without a chimney, he would have a right to do so only up to the centre-line. In so doing he would, naturally, also have to respect next-door's cross-easement in their flues. Indeed, it has been known for this unhappy arrangement only to be made apparent when next-door's live flue spouts smoke into the neighbour's fire-less house.

The alternative interpretation of the boundary in these circumstances is that it should run in zig-zag fashion around the flues. In the absence of documentary evidence, I refuse to believe such a hypothesis.

I will conclude this chapter by restating the norm. Usually, the boundary line between buildings with a common wall runs down the centre of that wall.

Chapter 9
The 'L'-shaped house

One of the most common layouts of housing which gives rise to doubt about the position of the boundary is the street full of L-shaped houses (Fig. 14).

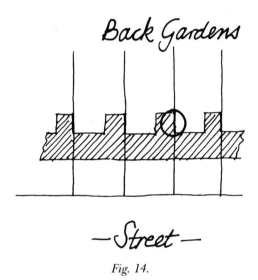

Fig. 14.

To many people it is obvious that since the wall of the rear extension forms part of their building, and only bounds the garden of next-door, the wall must belong to them. They are almost always wrong. Since the wall between the two gardens usually abuts the rear projection, and forms a continuation of the wall of the house, the error as to ownership of the house wall is frequently extended in similar fashion to produce a mistake about the garden wall as well.

Unfortunately this readily understandable confusion can give rise to a lot of ill-feeling between neighbours. Show the following illustration (Fig. 15) to any doubters, and perhaps they will understand.

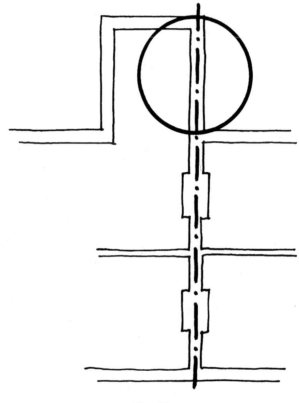

Fig. 15.

In the vast majority of cases, the wall of the rear extension is a continuation of the wall between the main parts of the houses. As we have seen in an earlier chapter, it is usually safe to assume that the boundary between the houses is the centre line of the dividing wall. Unless the deed plan shows a definite kink – and in all my experience I have only met one which did – the boundary can equally safely be assumed to continue in a straight line. Half the rear extension wall, therefore, sits on the land of the adjoining owner. It is, of course, essential to check that both the assumptions we have made are in fact correct. Look at the deeds to make sure that you are not dealing with the second known case in which the boundary does jink to one side, and take measurements to prove that the rear wall is a continuation of the main one – or isn't, for that matter. If the deeds are straightforward – or, at any rate, straight – and the wall is likewise, then QED: the wall is a 'party' one.

Chapter 10

Garden walls, fences, and bits of string

As I said in the Introduction, there is an awful lot of trouble to be found in suburban back gardens. In this chapter I will try to provide some ideas on how to solve the problems which give rise to the trouble.

Before we get to some 'rules' for general guidance, I would point out that physical clues can be equally, perhaps more, helpful in providing evidence of ownership, and from ownership you can often proceed to the position of the boundary. Look at the other walls, fences, or bits of string marking out the limits of the plot. If the rear fence and one side fence appear to be of the same date and the same construction, that is *prima facie* evidence that the same chap built and owns them. If all the walls in a street have the buttresses on their eastern side, that tends to indicate that each house owns one wall, and its neighbour the other. If a wall goes right round three sides of a garden in one style, it was probably put up by and belongs to the owner of that garden. Now to generalities.

There are a number of general rules about walls and fences and how they relate to boundaries. Unfortunately, people being what they are, you will often find that suburbanites have ignored the rules in putting up their walls and fences, so that if you make assumptions based on generalities you will often be led astray. However, we must at least consider those rules, so that we have some sort of starting point.

I must emphasise here and now that there are all sorts of exceptions to these rules, and that to rush off to court on the basis of them alone would be extremely injudicious. Later in this chapter I will explain why.

If a garden wall has buttresses on one side only, it is probable that the wall belongs to the owner on whose side the buttresses are. The boundary is usually then the face of the wall furthest from the piers (Fig. 16). If the wall has symmetrical piers it is probably built astride the boundary, which runs down the centre of the wall.

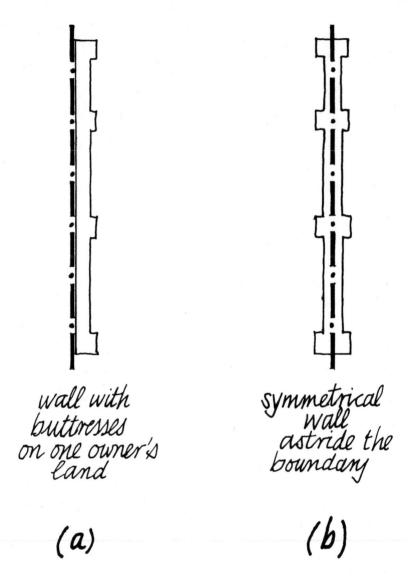

wall with
buttresses
on one owner's
land

symmetrical
wall
astride the
boundary

(a)

(b)

Fig. 16.

When a fence is constructed of posts, arris rails, and feather-edged boarding, it certainly used to be the case that the face of the boarding furthest from the rails marked the boundary. The logic behind this was that the space between the posts remained in the garden of the man who constructed the fence (Fig. 17), and it also used to be said that it was proper for a man to drive nails (through the boards) towards his own land. The counter-argument is that you can't construct such a fence, or repair it, without at least swinging

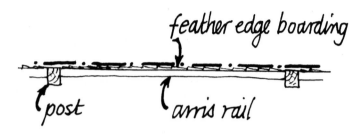

feather edge boarding

post   arris rail

(a)   Plan of post & rails fence

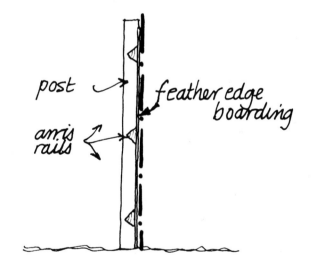

post

feather edge boarding

arris rails

(b) Section through post & rails fence

Fig. 17.

a hammer over the land of your neighbour and that (see elsewhere) you have no automatic right to do.

One leading authority, when asked for guidance on establishing the ownership of garden walls, replied: 'If it's in bad condition, it's next-door's.'

It is a standard presumption on OS maps, if not in law, and probably fairly safe in a field, that where there is a hedge – and no ditch, but then it would be unlikely to have one in a suburban garden – the boundary is the centre of the hedge.

If a fence consists of posts and wire, it's very likely to have been erected on the boundary. The thinner the divider, the more likely – on the whole – it is to be on the dividing line (Fig. 18).

That's most of the standard types of dividing wall (using the word loosely) that you're likely to find between back gardens. Of course, there are other types, the pseudo ranch-fencing in plastic, woven panels supported in various ways, or concrete boards dropped into slotted concrete posts, for example, but I wouldn't say that any of them had produced a presumption. Their position in relation to the true boundary will have to be deduced from first principles which, despite all the 'rules', is often the only safe way. I shall now point out why some of the presumptions are unsafe.

One very good reason for not assuming without question that a boundary feature follows the general rule is that the person who put it there may not have been aware of the rule. Another is that the constructor may have known the rule, but deliberately not followed it for some reason. Circumstances may have dictated a non-standard solution. Let us look at some of the rules, and likely eccentric variations.

A very simple, and frequent, deviation from the buttressed wall occurs when an unsupported wall starts to lean, and the party towards whom it starts to decline puts in piers to stop it going any further. These are usually fairly easily detected, since they tend not to be bonded into the wall, while piers contemporary with the wall usually are. Be warned that the reverse may be the case in either sort, and that even when you have solved the dating question, you're still only dealing with assumptions.

Feather-edged boarding is frequently to be found facing towards the man who owns the fence. He's paid for it, and he wants to see the pretty side. Besides which, he doesn't get on with the neighbours and he can put it up this way round without going on to their land to nail the boarding. When this happens, there's almost

38

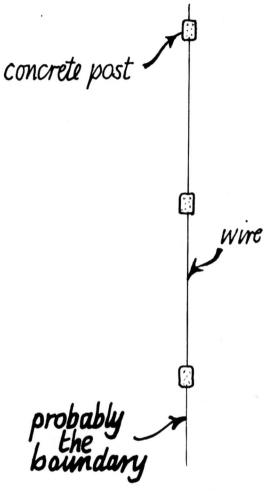

concrete post

wire

probably
the
boundary

Fig. 18.

always going to be a row, sometime, about where the boundary is. If
our man puts the boarding on the boundary, most of the posts will
be in the next door garden. If he puts the edge of the posts on the
boundary, then when he's finished erecting the fence a substantial
area of his garden will now be more accessible to his unloved neighbours. They'll be happy for now, but when he wants his land back
for any reason, they won't be quite so accommodating (Fig. 19).

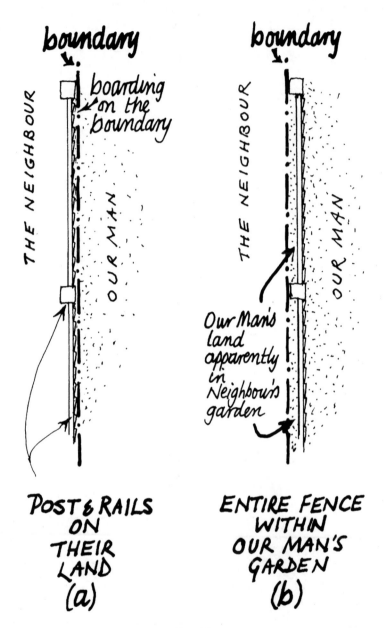

boundary

THE NEIGHBOUR

boarding on the boundary

OUR MAN

POST & RAILS
ON
THEIR
LAND
(a)

boundary

THE NEIGHBOUR

Our Man's land apparently in Neighbour's garden

OUR MAN

ENTIRE FENCE
WITHIN
OUR MAN'S
GARDEN
(b)

Fig. 19.

Hedges are frequently grown by one owner, because he likes them, and so they are grown entirely within his garden. Any attempt to move the boundary across to the centre of the hedge is likely to encounter opposition from the planter. Unfortunately, even when a fence already exists, when one owner grows a substantial hedge, the fence on the other owner's side becomes less important and, indeed, is often damaged by the growth. It either falls down or is taken down, and later owners may not know of its former existence. I have a current case in which both sides originally claimed that they (or their predecessors) had planted and owned the hedge, and by the time that one side had conceded the position of the hedge there was enough grist in the mill for a full-blooded and expensive trial of some far more trivial issues.

Almost always, however, the reason that the fence and the boundary cannot be safely assumed to be correctly conterminous or following the rules is human fallibility. Save for adverse possession (which see) the boundary does not move with the fence, but fences move all over the place, with time, weather, handymen, and even fencing contractors. Very, very rarely – despite what your client will tell you – do the neighbours deliberately try to steal some of next-door's garden. But they're very bad at putting fences back where they got them from.

My advice then, is: don't assume from presumptions; don't rely on anything that could have moved; don't believe anything that's been erected more recently than the houses; and work from fixed points wherever possible. Those fixed points are dealt with elsewhere.

Chapter 11

Hedges and ditches

Hedges and ditches give rise to frequent misunderstandings by lay-men, but produce an eloquent logicality in their relationship to boundaries in the eyes of the law – at least in one set of circumstances. In all others, the lack of a logical explanation means that other evidence must be sought.

Where there is a bank and a ditch between two properties, whether or not the bank has a fence or a hedge on it (it usually does have the latter), the presumption is that a man has walked to the limit of his ownership, dug his spade in, and thrown the earth up on to his own land. The far edge of the ditch is therefore the boundary (Fig. 20).

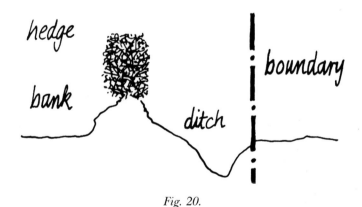

Fig. 20.

Of course, in time the edge of the ditch (like the Rockies) may crumble, eating into the land of the neighbour, but it is unlikely that the amount of movement which this would produce would be very significant in a field. It's not likely to happen in a suburban

43

back garden, where a few inches might matter. (See the chapter on 'How large is too little?')

When there is no bank, there is nothing to indicate how the ditch came into existence, and therefore no basis for any assumptions. If the ditch was quite clearly linked to drainage ditches or other features on one party's land, it might be reasonable, in the absence of contrary evidence, to assume that the ditch belonged to that party. Talking of drainage ditches reminds me of a case of mine where my client asked a contractor to dig such a ditch, well inside his own land, in which to lay a pipe. Shortly afterwards, a relation of the contractor bought the land next door, saw a few scrubby plants on her side of the boundary, and promptly took down the fence and re-erected it on the far side of the ditch, gaining about six feet by two hundred yards. The case continues. If there were two banks and one ditch, one might argue that the ditch had been a joint effort, and that the centre was the boundary.

Where there is a single bank, with no hedge or fence upon it, and no ditch on either side, you might again advance the 'joint effort' argument, but you should also look for any other evidence. Again, there is no legal presumption if the bank is between two ditches, but I would incline to the view that it would be reasonable to take the centre of the bank as the boundary.

Where there is a hedge alone, the OS practice is to take the middle of the hedge, but there is more likely to be supporting evidence for the ownership of a hedge, though its outward growth may give rise to arguments about the exact position of the boundary in relation to it. Such arguments are, on the whole, futile, and clients should be dissuaded from indulging in them, whenever possible. A surveyor may find it expedient to advise such clients to find another adviser, when only a couple of inches are at stake. There may be hedges on other sides of the land which were clearly planted by the same owner at the same time, and it is not unreasonable, then, to assume that all those hedges belong to, and stand on the land of, the same owner. Where OS field numbers are used in a conveyance, then the OS boundaries are those which should prevail, and whether or not they show physical features such as hedges which might, in other circumstances, have ditches to be conveyed with them, is irrelevant.

There is no substitute for using your eyes in this kind of situation, not only to read the deeds but also to assemble all the visual evidence. Then you have to apply your brain to put all the evidence together. I was called in to a case where the evidence on site was very confused, and where there was a holly hedge of considerable age and thickness. One side was attempting to argue that the far side of the holly hedge formed the boundary – at least where the hedge existed. Embedded in the hedge, however, was an iron fence which looked to me like the sort which is used to separate the immediate surroundings of stately homes from the farm lands adjoining. Furthermore, the wood of the holly had in places grown around the iron so as to enclose it totally. I therefore argued that the fence had clearly come first, marking the boundary, and that the hedge had come later, grown up around it, and had no relevance to the position of the boundary at all. Later on, an early plan turned up which showed the pleasure grounds of a large house on one side of the boundary, and a field on the other: this made the iron fence an even more likely candidate.

I should perhaps end this chapter by saying, since I said it to myself each time I wrote a sentence which referred to a presumption, that all these cases assume that there is no positive evidence to the contrary. Even the best presumption, the bank and single ditch case, would be overturned by a clear statement in the deeds – especially if in deeds on both sides of the ditch – that the boundary lay somewhere else.

Chapter 12

Streets

It has been said that there are two kinds of people in the world: those who divide things into two categories, and those who don't. Some of the distinctions drawn in other chapters of this book have been between walls formerly inside the London Building Acts and those outside. In this chapter, a similar but more restrictive distinction may be made: between those streets inside the City of London and those outside.

Outside the City, the doctrine of '*ad medium filum*' – to which the word '*viae*' is sometimes added – usually applies. That means that if you own land fronting on to a highway, you are deemed to own up to the middle of the street, even if it is not shown on the deed plan or mentioned in the conveyance. While the road continues to function, the highway authority owns as much of the surface and topsoil (if that's the right word) of the land as is necessary for their statutory operations, and the public has all its customary rights to use the road.

When a road is closed, however, the ownership reverts to the frontager. I say 'reverts', because the assumption which justifies allowing the owner to take possession of half the road width is that he gave it up in the first place – or his primordial ancestor did – in order to allow the road to be formed. If you can get a road stopped up, then, you can add enormously to your plot and thence to your potential development.

This practice derives from legal presumption, and is not an invariable rule. Actual facts may displace the presumption, such as the outright sale of the land for the road, by the frontager to the authority. The existence of vaults under the street, on the other hand, will strongly support a claim to the ownership beneath the road.

Vaults may be relevant in connection with the second of our two categories: streets inside the City of London. Most of those streets are chartered, and the City owns them hook, line and sinker;

47

or, to put it another way, *usque ad coelum et ad inferos.* The frontager does not then own *ad medium filum* and, incidentally, is not therefore an adjoining owner to a building on the far side of the street, which he might be deemed to be if he were elsewhere than in the City.

Despite the City's ownership of the street, however, one can still own the vaults under them. Trevor Aldridge (to whose book on *Boundaries, Walls and Fences* I will give another plug here, in gratitude for the following story) relates that his firm's premises had lavatories in the vaults beneath a City street. When some doubt arose as to ownership of the vaults, his then senior partner made a statutory declaration that he had used the WCs, man and boy, for the past X years; and that the firm had thus acquired a squatter's (*sic*) title to them.

Chapter 13

Overhanging and underpinning

In London – that is to say, the part of it which was covered by the London Building Acts – it is usually fairly safe to assume that the face of the external wall of a building forms the boundary, rather than any imaginary line formed by projecting downwards from the eaves or upward from the foundations. The reason for this is that the 1939 Amendment Act (and its predecessors, for that matter) specifically gave a right to cut off any projections of that sort, when it was necessary to do so in order for a building owner to erect his own wall on the boundary. This seems to assume (and we all know how dangerous assumptions are, don't we?) that a man will get the maximum enclosure for his building that he can, and hope to get away for as long as possible with the additional projections.

Although S.54 of the 1939 Act stated that the Act does not "authorise any interference with any easement ... relating to a party wall", it can be argued that not only do the express provisions of S.46 (1)(h) (which deal with cutting off projections) override the generality of the later section, but also that such projections are usually attached to an independent wall, rather than a party one. The Party Wall etc. Act, 1996 will produce much the same effect.

The right to cut off projections would also seem to exclude by implication the possibility that adverse possession (see the eponymous chapter) might be claimed in respect of land between footings and eaves. You'd have to do something far more exclusive to make such a presumption stick. In other words, mere ownership of elements above and below someone else's land will not give you any chance of claiming the space between.

It is quite clear at common law that when you sell a building with such projecting features, the whole of the building passes from vendor to purchaser, even if the land is correctly described and shown as being limited to the face of the wall. This is expressly confirmed by *Truckell* v. *Stock*, 1957. The air space between the projections remains in the ownership of next door and, following the

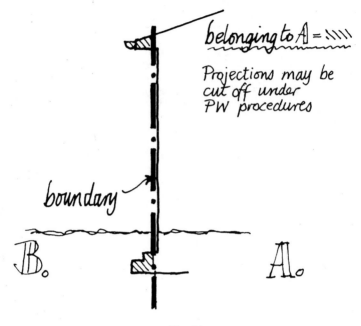

Fig. 21.

new Party Wall Act, you can no longer acquire an easement to have
your eaves and your foundations projecting into next-door's land,
without the fear of losing (Fig. 21).

Next door to a church in Hampstead I once encountered an
adjoining owner who dug up an obscure case to prove – as he
thought – that he did own the land above his projecting footings,
and no amount of argument or exposition of the law would persuade him otherwise. In the end, I advised the church to carry on
building up to what we were all convinced was the boundary (the
face of his wall) and see whether he was prepared to put his money
where his mouth was. He wasn't.

Overhanging trees present a different sort of problem. The law
as to responsibility for a tree's actions is quite straightforward. Whoever planted it stops the buck – or his successor in title does. Very
often the roots and branches of a tree will bridge the boundary, but
sometimes even its trunk does. Since, as every schoolboy used to
know, 'Great oaks from little acorns grow', a sapling planted clearly

on one side of an infinitely thin line can easily grow into a tree straddling that line, with a substantial amount of wood on each side of it.

I had a case once which started as a 'damage' case, and turned into a boundary one. My client's house was somewhere on the north side of London, and had belonged to a famous wartime Air Vice Marshal, or some such. The house next door was complaining that its west wing – to put it rather too grandly: it was really the kitchen extension, with a bedroom over it – was being attacked by the roots of my client's giant oak. There was no doubt about the damage, and very little about the cause of it; the bill was going to be substantial.

In the course of my discussions with the client, it emerged that the neighbours had proposed to chop down the tree, and my client had refused to allow them to do so, claiming the tree as his own. When I asked why it had been necessary to 'claim' it, I was told that the boundaries were very uncertain in that area: there was a public footpath between 'our' grounds and 'their' garden. Careful examination of the deeds and the local council's plans revealed that, although parts of the tree were certainly within my client's land, it could well be argued that the seed had originally fallen out-side.

I suggested saying so. 'But I love that tree, protested my client, 'and they might chop it down.' 'Which', I asked him, 'would you prefer: losing the tree or paying the damages?'

We disclaimed the tree, the action for damages was withdrawn, and I sent in my bill based, as always, on time expended, with nothing extra for the ingenuity I had displayed on behalf of my client. It will come as no surprise to those of you versed in the ingrati-tude of clients that he refused to pay my bill in full, supported by his solicitor, because he could not see how I had spent so much time on the job. I had, of course, spent a lot of time on the claim before I discovered that there might be a cheaper way out for my client: much cheaper, since he bilked me as well.

If overhanging branches or projecting roots cause offence to the neighbour, he can lop them off as long as he offers anything cut off back to the owner. Like Shylock, he must be careful not to cut one iota beyond the permitted limits. He can also, in appropriate cases, seek an injunction to restrain the offending objects from growing. Since trees are notorious for failing to observe the dictates of the court, their owner will have to comply on their behalf.

A Tree Preservation Order applies to the whole tree, so an adjoining owner cannot use self-help on a protected tree. I'm not sure where that leaves him if the roots are causing damage, and I'm not even sure that it matters in this book, but if I find out before we go to press I'll add a footnote.[†]

I only included the word 'underpinning' in the title of this chapter for euphony's sake, but perhaps I can usefully add that before the passing of the Party Wall Act you had no right to underpin beyond the exact boundary of your property, which made dealing with a 'party' wall distinctly difficult, if you have an uncooperative neighbour. Nowadays, in England and Wales, you can underpin the whole wall, but you can't put reinforcement on the far side of the boundary unless your neighbour agrees.

[†] A friendly barrister tells me that your only recourse against an offending tree, protected by a TPO, would be to apply to the local authority for removal of the Order, or at least a variation sufficient to let you abate the damage-causing elements. What you do if they refuse, and whether an action would lie against the council, even he wasn't sure, but you could probably apply for judicial review of their decision.

Chapter 14

Horizontal boundaries

There is a general presumption in English law that *'cuius est solus eius est usque ad coelum et ad inferos.'* This may be roughly translated as meaning that if you own the land, you own everything under it and over it.

To illustrate the effect of this, I can tell you about a redevelopment that certain property magnates were wanting to carry out. They owned a five-storey building, let out in many small tenancies. They had succeeded in buying out all the tenants except one, who held a ground floor shop together with its small back yard. The new building was intended to be deeper than the old (i.e. to measure more from front to back), and my clients therefore proposed to preserve the single obstinate tenant in place while they constructed their new office block over, round, and behind him. They were deeply distressed to be told that they could not develop over the shop's back yard because, no vertical limitation having been placed on the demise, all the air space above the yard had also been let to the tenant. They could have coped with the shop, but not with the yard as well, so that removal of the tenant became essential, instead of just highly desirable. Fortunately, the party wall surveyor (whom modesty, etc.) was able to persuade the tenant of the advantages of moving.

There have been one or two cases in the courts where this failure to limit a demise vertically has led to disputes as to the ownership of roof space. In those which I have read, the failure by the landlord specifically to limit the tenancy to a particular point above the flat, such as the top of the ceiling joists, has led to a finding by the court that the tenants were entitled to use the space in the roof above their ceiling for storage.

In *Haines* v. *Florensa* (reported by Barry Denyer-Green in 1989 EGCS86), the demise of the top flat included the top surface of the ceiling to the lower flat, and the roof. It was held that there was an implication that the airspace above the flat had been demised, and that therefore the tenant was entitled to raise the roof and convert the loft to provide additional living space.

I think that we can safely say, then, that the legal position of the top element in any structure is fairly straightforward – insofar as one can ever be sure that anything is definite in the law where, it seems to me, the quixotic decisions of the courts are far more likely to vary than the advice given by a competent surveyor. Unless an upper limit is specifically set by a legal document, the owner owns, or the tenant leases, everything upwards from his holding.

The situation is far less clear when you have an upper and a lower hereditament. It has been held that the demise of a flat must extend upwards at least as far as the underside of the joists to which the ceiling is attached, but no similar decision has come to my attention in a downwards direction. Logic suggests that the top of the joists to which the floorboards are fixed must be the minimum extent to which an upper flat will read downwards.

I know of no decision about ownership of, or responsibility for, the joists between the upper and the nether millstone. It might be reasonable to assume that, in the absence of specific words to the contrary, each party would own up to (or down to) half-way; but it would probably be safer to assume that, if you made any such presumption, the courts would upset it.

The lesson to be learnt – and indeed which seems to be being learned by latter-day lessors – is that it is highly desirable that the parties should make their intentions clear in any lease of a property which is adjacent to another vertically above or below it. It is, of course, desirable always, but especially so when there are no presumptions to help.

Under the Party Wall etc. Act, there are such things as party floors/ceilings. Unfortunately, their existence still doesn't help to decide ownership, but ownership may not matter quite so much when the apportionment of the cost of works to any party structure can be decided using the mechanism of the Act.

Under the London Building Acts, the occurrence of horizontal party structures was limited, and that was because they were stated only to be within the definition when the properties were 'approached solely by separate staircases or separate entrances from without'. This meant that while the converted basement flat of a Victorian mansion might well have a separate entrance from, and thus a party ceiling/floor with, the ground floor flat, all the upper flats were likely to be reached via the original front door. In a modern block of flats, it may well be that none of the flats enjoyed a horizontal party structure.

A working party set up by the Pyramus and Thisbe Club (for a full description of that partly learned society of party wall surveyors, see *Party Walls and what to do with them*) felt that this was an invidious distinction, and in drafting the new Party Wall etc. Act, declared that separate front doors were enough. The removal of a need for a separate entrance from the street means that a large part of the horizontal problem has been removed, but even the existence of such Utopian conditions does not remove the advisability of expressing clearly the extent of any property being dealt with by sale or lease.

There are a number of exceptions to the general rule of '*cuius est*' with which I began this chapter. Certain minerals are auto-matically reserved to various bodies. Coal, for example, belongs to the National Coal Board – if it still exists by the time these words are printed; gold and silver belong to the Crown, following an Eliza-bethan (the First) case.

Overflying is permitted by Act of Parliament, and in a recent case it was held that even quite low flying, for the purpose of aerial photography, could not be prevented as an act of trespass or the invasion of privacy.

It is this last case which gives some hope that the Anchor Brew-houses case might be reversed. Since '*cuius est, eius est*', a crane may not be swung over a neighbour's land without his consent. Under the previous leading case, *Woollerton and Wilson v. Costain*, the words 'which shall not be unreasonably withheld' had effectively been added. Woollerton had applied for an injunction to restrain Costains from swinging their crane over his land. Costains had offered all sorts of assurances and inducements to Woollerton, so the judge granted the injunction, but suspended its operation for long enough to enable Costains to complete their works.

From 1970 onwards, then, a nice balance existed. Developers knew that if they treated adjoining owners fairly, they were likely to be allowed to swing their cranes, and the neighbours knew that if they were unreasonable in their demands, they might find that they couldn't hold the builder to ransom. During this happy period, one such case came through my hands. A grasping neighbour demanded £150,000 for allowing the crane to swing, and I advised the distraught contractor to offer £5,000 in an open letter, with all the usual safeguards for the adjoining property, and to say that if this was rejected they would swing anyway, and see him in court. He took the money.

In 1987, however, Anchor Brewhouses succeeded in obtaining an immediate injunction to prevent Berkley House from swinging their cranes over the plaintiff's land. The court affirmed the '*cuius, eius*' doctrine, but said, *obiter*, that there were strong arguments for limiting its upward application to a height which any reasonable man on the Clapham skyscraper might need for the proper enjoyment of his property. I think that this may well come, and in the third edition of this book a lot of this chapter may be replaced by a statement to the effect that a man's rights in his property cease twenty feet above the topmost physical part of his building.

To avoid any possible misunderstanding, I must stress that the last sentence is not a statement of the present state of the law, as I write in 1998.

Chapter 15

Finding the position of the dividing wall

What I am about to tell you must seem obvious, but knowledge of what I am about to impart would have saved some litigants of my acquaintance a great deal of money. You want to find the position of the dividing wall between your house and next door, and the centre of that wall. I am assuming, yet again, that the wall stands equally on the land of both parties, and that the boundary runs down the middle.

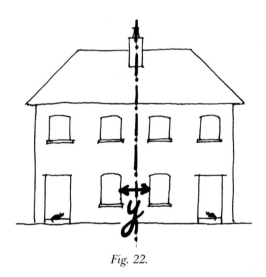

Fig. 22.

It is very easy to be confused in apparently simple cases, like Fig. 22, by drainpipes which come down somewhere near the boundary line between the two properties. Sometimes a drainpipe is cranked near the gutter for the express purpose of reaching the ground on one side of the boundary, so as to allow a fence to be constructed in the right place. To be certain of the correct position, measurements are necessary.

If this is a joint exercise, and your neighbour is being cooperative, this will all be very easy, as you will be measuring inside and outside both houses, and checking each other's work. Usually, unfortunately, this sort of exercise is being carried out because both parties are already at each other's throats because of a disagreement about the position of a fence.

May I recommend – though probably too late – that you should approach your neighbour and do the measuring before you erect or replace the fence?

If you are on speaking terms with next door, and your houses are symmetrical, you simply divide the distance between the two nearest identical features, and the result puts you in the middle, standing on the boundary. You can check this by carrying out the exercise shown in Fig. 23.

Find the nearest convenient hole in your own wall. By this I mean a window or a door in the rear or front wall of the house. Ideally, put something through it at right angles, i.e. parallel to the dividing wall. Measure from your marker to the inside face of the wall. Add on half an inch to an inch for plaster. This distance should give you the position of the brick face of the dividing wall. Now measure the same distance from your marker along the outside of the house, and you should have reached the same position: opposite the projection of the brick face of the dividing wall.

Now, if your neighbour's house is apparently symmetrical with yours, you can fairly safely assume that if you measure the distance between your respective doors (windows, or other holes) you will be able to ascertain the thickness of the wall. If you aren't friends with the neighbour, or if you don't want him to know you're carrying out this exercise, you may have to poke a measuring device over the fence while he's not looking. If you don't want to lean over, or it's too far, you can probably guess at a wall between 9 and 11 inches thick, and thus locate the boundary within an inch, working only from your own side.

If you can measure from both sides, $Y-2X' =$ thickness. In other words, from the total distance between the openings, subtract twice the distance you measured to find the face of the wall, and the result will be the thickness of the wall. The boundary, all other things being equal, will be in the centre of it.

If your houses are unbalanced (like most people think their

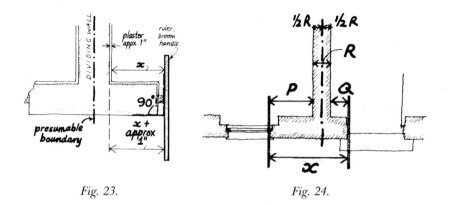

Fig. 23.   Fig. 24.

neighbours are, let alone their properties), as in Fig. 25, carry out
the exercise illustrated in Fig. 24. Again this can be an easy joint
exercise, or involve an assumption as to wall thickness.

In this case, the equation is $X - (P + Q) = R$, and the boundary
is therefore either at $P + \frac{1}{2}R$ from the left-hand window, or $Q + \frac{1}{2}R$
from the right-hand door. (If you're lucky, it will be both.)

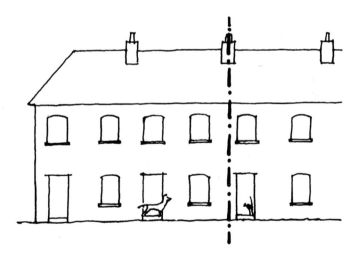

Fig. 25.

I say again that this may all seem obvious, but I've been to court on a number of cases where the contestants couldn't even agree upon this apparently self-evident starting point.

I had a case in Harrow where the other side had pushed (literally) their garden shed across the boundary, right up against my client's rear extension, which he had constructed so as to leave space for maintenance between the wall and the boundary. It took a county court action to persuade next door to pull their shed back to the 'party wall' line. More recently, I sat as arbitrator on a case where one side argued that a cranked drainpipe 'proved' that the boundary was more in their favour than the other side were prepared to concede. They appeared to have overlooked completely the fact that the drainpipe on the front of the house argued against them to exactly the same extent.

The position of the centre-line of the wall is of great importance when we consider fences and walls in the garden, while if your neighbour is so stupid as to want to ruin his house (and the neighbourhood) with stick-on stone, you certainly don't want him coming half an inch on to your side of the boundary.

Chapter 16

The empty garden

A tomb without a body in it is called a cenotaph; a wall without a window is said to be imperforate; what do you call a garden without a fence? I only ask, because that would have made a better title for this chapter than the one I have chosen. What I am going to examine is how you should set about deciding the line of a fence between two gardens, when there isn't one, and you have been called in to advise on how and where it should be built.

The lack of a fence, wall, what-have-you, may have arisen in a number of ways. Perhaps the estate developer left it to the purchasers to erect a fence, and the two neighbours – or their children – got on so well together that they preferred to have the use in common of double the space. Now one or both of the original owners have moved, and the new ones would like their properties demarcated. Or perhaps the fence fell down (or blew down in one of those hurricanes that the weather forecasters are so dismissively sure aren't coming our way) so thoroughly that its original position can no longer be ascertained with certainty.

Even if a former fence has left some posts or some post-holes behind it, there may be considerable debate about which side of the posts the boundary lies (see the chapter on Garden walls, fences, and bits of string), or whether the posts are or were in the right place to start with (see the chapter on Adverse possession). However, with or without residual evidence, you're going to have to start somewhere.

If your client will allow it, the first thing you should do is talk to the owner of the garden on the other side of the missing fence. I have emphasised the importance of this elsewhere, but it must be repeated. If you agree on the line of the fence before it is put up, there is less chance (not none) of your being asked to take it down or move it later. For the purposes of this chapter, let us assume that your neighbour is ignorant but co-operative: he's not going to obstruct you, but he hasn't got any definitive help to offer.

First of all, look at both deeds. With any luck at all, they will both be based on the same OS extract, and may even be the same plan with a different part ringed in red. If that is the case and they look something like the next illustration (Fig. 26), your task should be fairly straightforward. No. 25, next door, bears the same dimensions and so, despite my distrust of deed plan measurements, you can start from the fence with No. 21 and measure to the fence with No. 27, and see how close you get to sixty feet. If it's bang on, you can safely take thirty feet as your garden width.

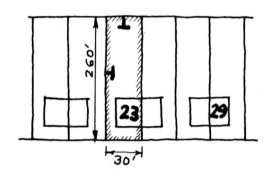

Fig. 26.

But, as I have already stated, the centre of the party wall must be an absolutely fixed boundary, so what if the distance from the fence is not thirty feet to that point? Prefer the wall, but don't assume that the rest of the boundary should necessarily shift by the same amount. In such a case, I would divide the bottom of the gardens at the thirty foot mark (or as near to it as possible), and take a straight line from there to the centre line of the wall.

In the past few paragraphs, I have rather been thinking in terms of back gardens. Front gardens are often more tricky, because shared drives can make it more difficult to find a starting point for any measurement. You have the safe starting point of the centre of the wall and, in a simple case, you should be able to project it forward by triangulation, to continue the straight line of the wall. This does rather rely on the builder having set the house out squarely in the first place. I would rather proceed to a fixed point on the front boundary, if I could find one to rely on.

Ownership of the right-hand fence to No. 23 is almost certainly, in the case we're looking at, with No. 25. His deeds may show it, if we have access to them, but the 'T' mark on our left-hand boundary implies it anyway. If there are no 'T' marks to be seen, you will have to wander a little further afield: *viz.* next door but one, two, and so on, to see if there is an established pattern of fencing to indicate ownership. Remembering that they are only indications, you can nevertheless reasonably assume that if the nine nearest gardens all have the fencing facing one way, the missing one should face the same way and may well belong to the party to whom the standard assumptions would point.

You should, of course, look for indications on the ground. Old fence-post holes, signs of attachment of the fence at the junction with the house, and at both ends of the garden. These may be even more necessary when you are dealing with irregular boundaries between unequal plots.

Once again, if you can compare the deeds, do so. You may need to enlarge one or the other, and make overlays to compare or join them, but at least that is comparatively easy nowadays, with photocopiers that will do it for you to a high degree of accuracy – even if you shouldn't rely on 97% to mean exactly what it says as a reduction factor. If it is dangerous, by the way, to scale off a small deed plan, it is positively suicidal to do so off a photocopy. Don't.

I have always said that you must never put in print the fact that real experts know when to break the rules, because it encourages amateurs to do so when they shouldn't. It is with great reluctance therefore that I admit to having scaled off some blown-up photocopies in an attempt to solve a boundary problem in Harrow on one occasion. (This is a different case from any others in Harrow mentioned in this book.) Only one dimension was given on the plan, and virtually no measurements scaled from it agreed with any taken on site – including the one given. I therefore attempted to get some acceptable proportions from a big blow-up. They all bore some resemblance to each other, and to the facts on site. I didn't rely on them. Don't you.

When married, the two deeds should agree along the common boundary. If they don't, you have a serious problem on your hands, and you will either have to reach a friendly agreement with the neighbour, which should then be recorded on both deeds in legal form, and notified to the Land Registry, or face the costly consequences. Failure to agree may produce the absurdly expensive legal proceedings to which I have alluded elsewhere. I say yet again: it is better to give up a few inches of garden than to pay for several days in court.

When the overlaid plans agree, you still have the problem of identifying the boundary on the ground. Use every fixed point you can lay your hands on, and work from one to another as far as possible.

Lack of evidence is also positive assistance sometimes. I was able to assert positively, in one case, that if a fence had been fastened anywhere in such and such an area there would be signs of it. There were no signs, therefore the old position of the fence – and hence the boundary – had to be to one side of that area. Thus, the boundary was 'not to the left of point A'.

Sometimes there will be very little in the way of evidence on the ground. There were two front gardens in Wembley, separated by a hedge. The deeds showed a boundary with an angle in it, but nowhere near enough measurements to be able accurately to fix the point at which the bend occurred (Fig. 27).

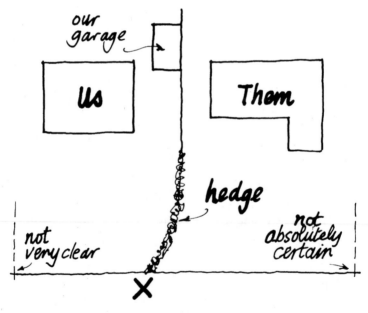

Fig. 27.

64

When I was called in, 'they' had pulled up the hedge completely, leaving 'our' garage as the only point of certainty: the boundary was 'not to the left of' our garage. We had dimensions for the front of each plot, but neither of the opposite corners gave crystal clear starting points. Doing the best we could, however, got us to a more or less reliable point 'X'. From there to the garage we knew very little more than you can see in the diagram, but the further from the street the bend came, the better it suited 'them', since they might just be able to get a car past the house, which they couldn't with the hedge there.

Not for the first time, aerial photographs were of considerable assistance. Even quite obscure suburban properties may appear in such photos, and the cost of obtaining them can be much less than that of a day in court. We could see the line of the former hedge quite clearly, could roughly trace its centre-line, and could relate that to our two fixed points. We were able to satisfy ourselves and, after some considerable time, our reluctant neighbours, where the boundary was in relation to where the hedge used to be. We were even able, by extrapolation from other ground features, coupled with what measurements we could place some reliance on, to determine where the bend came.

The more uncertainty there is on the ground and the plans, the more important it is to stay out of court. If you can see that the issue is not clear-cut, you must realise that there is a case to be made for some other point of view. If you and your neighbour each find a surveyor to share your opinion, the two surveyors will both be subjected to lengthy cross-examination, the result may well be a toss-up anyway, and the judge will sum up by saying: 'The true view is this.' As I have said in another connection, this means: 'I have heard a lot of argument; I don't understand half of it, and don't agree with the other half; what I think is. ...'

What a waste of money. Avoid it if at all possible by reaching a compromise. If you have to give something, console yourself with the thought that you're probably getting something as well. And just think of all the hi-fi equipment, records and discs you'll be able to buy with what you've saved on legal expenses. On the other hand, there are quite a few records I would still like to acquire, so if you're set on confrontation, you can either instruct me or suggest my name to your opponent.

Chapter 17

The task of the expert witness

Originally, according to a talk given at a Building Surveyors' Weekend Briefing, the task of the expert witness was to assist the court, and to that end he was appointed by the court. Nowadays, each side appoints their own expert, and they argue unhelpfully in front of the judge. Of course, experts do differ and there are cases where honest disagreements can occur, but too often the witness seems to see it as his duty to be a kind of secondary advocate.

This kind of attitude is seen at its worst in planning enquiries, where the Local Authority witness, nine times out of ten, will end his proof of evidence by inviting or urging the Inspector to dismiss the appeal. This is no part of the job of the witness. He is there to use his expertise – of which much will be made by his counsel – to lay facts and, where appropriate, opinion before the court. It is for counsel to tell the court what conclusions are to be drawn from the facts, and to urge the judge to see things from his side's point of view. The crucial distinction is between giving evidence of truth and using advocacy to urge a particular decision.

If you are asked to give evidence in a boundary dispute you should not seek to support your client's view – certainly not initially. You should approach the question dispassionately, and try to arrive at the truth. If your report supports the client, he may well employ you to appear on his behalf. If it does not, you should submit an account for your work to date, and bow out: you should not look for a way in which you can alter your view of the facts in order to please your client. What is more, do not be afraid to tell your client that he is wasting his time – and yours. I heard of a case where a surveyor was asked to deal with an infringement of two inches caused by a thickset hedge, and I understand that he told the instructing solicitor to get lost. A man after my own heart: there are too few of us about.

Similarly, if there are points for and points against your side, you should not attempt to conceal them, certainly not when under cross-examination. Anstey's first rule of being cross-examined is: when asked a damaging question, give the answer straight off, without hedging. Leave it to your counsel to extract from you in re-examination why this is not really damaging to your general conclusion.

A textbook example of this occurred in a recent boundary dispute case of mine. In my opinion, the boundary was a more or less straight line, definitely running along the remains of an iron fence, and meeting the corners of two other properties, one at either end. I said that those properties had been there for ages, and that they therefore gave certainty to the two ends of the line. A discrepancy between two OS maps, one of 1936/8 and the other of 1960/9 was pointed out to me, showing that the garden at one end had certainly moved. Did I agree that this cast doubt upon my theory? 'Yes', was my reply. Then I was asked to project the line of the fence shown on a survey plan of the mid-1980s. Where did that come at the opposite end? 'About two feet away from where I say it should', I answered. In re-examination counsel asked me if either of those matters disturbed my general conclusion, and I said emphatically that they did not.

Space does not permit me to reproduce in full the cross-examination of the other side's expert on the second of those questions. Although the projected line did not meet the corner of the neighbouring garden, as I said that the boundary did, it came a lot closer to my view of the true boundary than that of my opponent, which is why he, too, was asked the question, but using his own survey plan. 'Please project a line through the fence on your plan towards the garden, Mr X.' 'I don't think that it is a proper line to draw.' Counsel: 'Never mind what you think, Mr X, just draw the line.' 'I don't think it is safe to draw a line through such a short length of fence.' Counsel: 'I understand your reservations, Mr X, but please just carry out the exercise.' 'This piece of fence is only about eight metres long in a boundary of about forty-five metres. You can't draw conclusions from that.' Counsel: 'I'm not asking you to draw conclusions, Mr X, just the line.' And so on for about ten minutes before, very reluctantly, the witness drew the line and admitted that it came very close to the point of the garden.

The result of behaviour like this is to convince the judge that you have something to hide, in not answering the question first time, and to throw into doubt the honesty of your whole approach. By contrast, if you honestly admit the flaws and defects in your client's case (not your case, remember: you're not making a case, just giving evidence), you are much more likely to be believed when you say that something is definitely so.

You should always be careful to distinguish between facts, well-supported opinion, and guesses. For example, in the question of a back garden boundary, you can know where the centre of the wall between the houses is, you can be pretty certain that the boundary starts from that point, and you can guess that it carries on in a straight line through any other point whose position can be well established. Make the strength of your certainty known to the court: contrary to what some witnesses seem to think, doubt and hesitancy when you are not sure will actually work in your favour.

I am very fond of quoting from my own experience. This is not just done to demonstrate to you how wonderful I am – you can find that out in other ways. It is because I find that actual cases make the best examples, and those that I have been involved in have taught me the most, so that I try to share that learning experience with my readers. This is by way of a prelude to my next example.

There was a boundary in Harrow where a first-floor extension over a rebuilt garage had been erected by one side, and a new fence had started (nearly finished) being put up by the other side. When my clients refused to allow the last few yards of fence to be swung, as they saw it, well into their garden, the other side sued for a declaration that the fence went where they said it did and, for good measure, that the garage extension was trespassing as well. This latter was despite the fact that my clients had consulted their neighbours about the position of the garage, and had even set it four inches further into their own garden when the line was questioned.

By the time I came on the scene, there was very little original evidence. The garage had been built, the old fence was long since gone, and the new fence was up for 90% of its length. All that remained were one or two old post holes at the rear, one or two old posts at the front, and some permanent structures on my clients' side of the boundary. There was therefore a lot of evidence about which I had to make all sorts of caveats, but I could say, for example, that I was sure that the concrete foundations of my clients' pond and of their shed had been there for some considerable time. About other matters I was less sure, and said so.

One particular matter stands out in my memory of this case. At the very end of the garden, where the proposed encroachment had so aroused the wrath of my clients, there was all sorts of evidence to show where the old fence had not been, but none to show where it had. I refused, therefore, to say where exactly it had ended, but averred very positively that it could not have been 'to the left of point X', because the well-established creeper, the trellis on the rear fence, and a post of the fence separating the gardens from those of the next street, which had no signs of an erstwhile dividing fence having been attached to it, all indicated very firmly to me that the disputed fence had not been fixed there. I did not stay for the judgment, in order to minimise costs, but I am told that the judge said that Mr Anstey struck him as a witness who did not say he was certain of a thing unless he had good grounds for doing so. The result of this was that the court accepted in full the matters on which I had spoken with certainty, and generally accepted my opinion on others. Honesty is the best policy.

You will have noticed that there is a vein of conceit running through my books. That is partly there to impress my readers, but mostly to encourage me. It's a terrifying thing being an 'expert'. You are always expected to produce the goods, whereas the general practitioner who lays claim to no special expertise can always escape, when the going gets tough, by saying: 'I think this is getting a little beyond me, and we ought to call in an expert'.

I am frequently scared stiff, and very often because I'm sure I'm right, and so can't see why the other side are going on. What have I missed, what are they suddenly going to hit me with in cross-examination? Those are the sort of thoughts that keep running through my head as a trial date approaches. I always go back to the site on the morning of a case, be it trial, arbitration, or planning enquiry, if I possibly can. It's so much better to have the whole thing clearly in your mind from a recent inspection, and you often see something on that very last check. As it happens, in the Harrow case, I made an extra visit on the morning to which the case had been adjourned, and saw something which nobody had spotted on the official court 'view'. Cross-examining counsel didn't like my answer and tried hard to shake me, but as I had seen the significant piece of evidence only hours before, I was able confidently to stick to my point.

However scared you are, you must go on and do your best for your client's sake, and the sake of your reputation. Half way to Hereford, I sat in my car and read the papers relating to a case I was on my way to look at. It concerned the line of junction between two ancient buildings. When I saw how many people had already examined the site, including an expert on timber-framed buildings, without resolving the problem, I asked myself why I had been fool enough to take on the job. What was I going to find that all these others had missed, or failed to agree on? Duty called so, despite my reluctance, I pressed on.

When I arrived, I had convinced myself that, since I was expected to know the answers, I jolly well had to find them. Spurred on by this, I succeeded in ascertaining that the timber-framed building owned, so to speak, all the frame that stood adjacent to the boundary. Walls had been set into it and up to it, and a few small bits of it had been cut away, but you could draw a line down the outside of all the main frame timbers and say: that is the boundary.

I was, as usual, very pleased with myself, but I was also extremely relieved. I really think that the essence of being an expert is to be constantly afraid of making the mistake that will ruin your reputation for ever, but nevertheless driving yourself on to put all your powers towards providing the expertise that is expected of you. When the fear becomes stronger than the will to succeed, it's time to retire and leave the field to younger men. Why do you think I'm writing all these books?

Well, not just yet.

Chapter 18

Clients

Do not let clients give evidence, if you can avoid it. I know it's their case, and there may be factual matters, or historical ones, on which they have to go into the witness box, but since all boundary disputes tend to have strong effects on the participants, the parties can become over-emotional when giving evidence, and damage their own cause. All surveyors know that their jobs would be easier to do if only clients weren't involved, but in boundary cases the adverse effect of this factor is at least doubled.

Big cases are usually much easier to deal with than little cases, and the size and standing of the clients is highly relevant, too. If Land Securities meet MEPC across a disputed boundary, they will appoint experienced surveyors and will, in all probability, accept their advice. The whole matter, involving city land worth hundreds of thousands of pounds, will be settled in a short time, between level-headed boards and their professional advisers.

I was once involved in a discussion (it was not a dispute: no one knew the facts, and both parties were united in their wish to reach an amicable and equitable solution) between a large foreign bank and a major land-owning charity. Between their two properties was an ancient wall, which clearly pre-dated both of the current buildings to which it was party. The bank was redeveloping, and wanted to use this opportunity to agree a boundary with the charity, to which the bank could build now and the charity later, without any future difficulty.

Both sides appointed competent surveyors, and the first thing they did was to commission an extremely accurate survey of the party wall. This produced an extraordinarily shaped thing, in both plan and section, which I have attempted to reproduce below (Fig. 28).

To our absolute delight, we discovered that there was one plane which could be drawn through the whole wall, which never stepped outside its thickness in plan or section, so we fixed on that

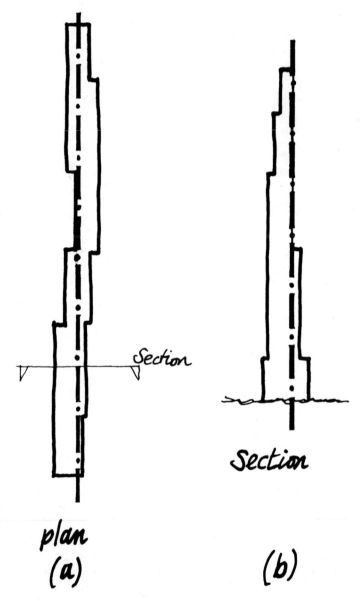

Section

Section

plan
(a)

(b)

Fig. 28.

as the boundary. The clients instantly agreed, and then all that had to be done was for the solicitors to enshrine it in a legal document. Explaining it to and teaching them was a different matter, but we got there in the end.

Let two suburban neighbours dispute which side of a fence post the boarding should be nailed, however, and you may be in for months – if not years – of ill-natured wrangling. One at least of the parties – not your side, of course – will have appointed an incompetent surveyor to advise them, or no surveyor at all. He may be the wife's brother-in-law, who's a quantity surveyor, or a clerk from the Borough Surveyor's office, or even a qualified surveyor who is so scared of offending one of the three paying customers he has at present that he daren't contradict them in anything, and certainly has no intention of applying his own limited powers to try to find out the truth of the situation.

It is very rarely that such disputes stop short of arbitration or the courts, and it would always have been cheaper for one party to pay the other for the disputed land, and often cheaper for one of them to move to another house to get away from the scene of the disagreement. Vain though the effort be, you must try to persuade your client, the sensible one, of the truth of these remarks, and try to get him to cut his losses.

If no powers of persuasion are of any avail, and the two parties cannot be brought to agreement, or even to a compromise in which both of them think themselves equally hard done by, then you must train your client in the art of giving evidence. (See the chapter on expert evidence for general remarks on the subject.) Impress upon him how important it is to stick to the subject of the dispute. Do not let him – or her – tell the court about the time when next door poisoned the roses (that was a case I had in Wales).

I was involved in a noise case in West London which was lost by an individual conducting his own case, when his expert's opinion was not unfavourable to his cause. He would insist on going over the planning history, emphasising how wrong it was that his neighbours had ever been given planning permission for the extension from which the noise emanated. Every time the Clerk of the Court dragged him back to the point, he would say: 'Yes, I see. Well, in 1972 when they applied for ...'. If he had kept his mouth shut, or better directed, and relied on his expert, I think he might well have won. As it was, he so exasperated the court that I clocked up another resounding triumph.

Even I have impossible clients, however. In the 1930s my father fished from the Thames a lady who had thrown herself in. He therefore became responsible for her (and later arrived home to find her, supposed to be baby-sitting in charge of your then infant author, just in time to stomach-pump her latest effort. In her favour, it has to be said that it was on her television set that I watched the Matthews' Cup Final of 1953). When she had a boundary dispute many years later, your author, by then grown to man's estate, was charged with sorting it out.

I didn't know, when the case started, that our client – I call her that: we didn't, of course, send in a bill – had earlier attacked the offending fence with a sledge-hammer, and had been bound over to keep the peace. I did, however, know the lady well enough to beg the solicitors to keep her out of the witness box: what could she add to my technical evidence? It's her case, they replied, and she wants to give evidence. I was cross-examined for two hours, and held firmly to my opinion. Then the client stepped into the box. 'It's like the Berlin Wall,' (it had just been built: when I originally wrote this chapter it was just coming down) she emoted. 'I don't promise I won't attack it again with my little sledge-hammer.' End of case.

Clients! Stay away from them. Keep them out of court. Keep them out of the witness-box. End of chapter.

Chapter 19

Mistakes I have made

Do not think that authors are infallible. It is well known that, if you read a newspaper report of an event which you attended, you will hardly recognise the matters described as being those which you witnessed. Contrary to the views expressed in *Lock up your Daughters* ('It must be true, for I read it in the papers, didn't you?'), something is not necessarily so because it is enshrined in print, and the author is not always right. (By the way, regular readers of mine may think that I have asked someone else to write this chapter, since I am generally believed to think that I am invariably correct about everything. However, this is me speaking.)

Still less should you assume that pundits never make mistakes in real life. They should, on the whole, get things right in a book, because another knowledgeable person will usually have checked the text. Only a very obstinate writer will persist in error, without at least pointing out that there is an alternative view. When you are actually involved in a case, however, it is not always easy to get an authoritative check on your opinion: the best person to go to – the one whom you would ask to read your manuscript – may be on the other side.

Some of the mistakes I have made (perhaps I should say: that I know I have made) point a general lesson. Some just point out how easy it is to err.

In a built-up area, when you are looking at the facades of two adjoining buildings there is often a clear-cut division between the two: one may be faced in brick, and the other in stone. The boundary is therefore obviously the line of junction between the two.

Oh no it isn't. There are all sorts of reasons why one or the other material may project across the boundary. Just one is that the stone facing may mask the joint between the two properties, in order to give a more elegant effect (Fig. 29).

A party wall award (if one happens to exist) or some other such agreement between the owners may well record the true

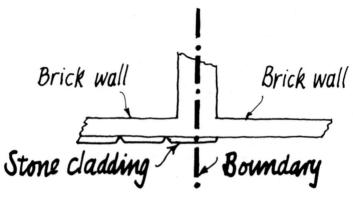

Fig. 29.

boundary, and perhaps state that the adjoining owner may cut off
the projecting stonework if he needs to do so when he comes to
redevelop.

A rather more excusable error is almost the reverse of that
case, but in some ways parallel. You can see a straight brick joint
between the two facades, and you therefore assume that there are
two walls behind the joint.

Not necessarily there aren't. Very often the joint has only been
put there to give an apparent dividing line, and it does not reflect
either the existence of two walls or the boundary. To make this mistake (Fig. 30) can be very embarrassing when you start to knock
down 'your' building. This happened to me on the site where the
Estates Gazette office now stands.

I must admit that I didn't make the next mistake: the other
side did, but I might have done if my client hadn't pointed it out to
me. If you are in possession of the plan of a newly-developed group
of plots, and the dimension from the outside of your wall to the
boundary is shown on the plan, then whatever next door says, that
dimension must be correct.

Well, not invariably it mustn't. On the plan, the distance from
the wall to the boundary was shown as two feet, but then so it was
on the other side of the line. The distance between the faces of the
two walls was only three feet nine inches. Either wall might be in
the wrong place, or the boundary might still be equidistant from
both. It turned out, for a very obvious reason when you looked

78

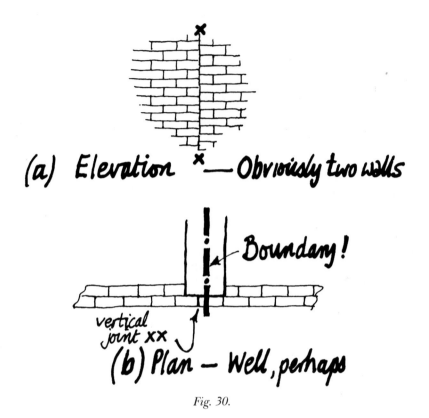

(a) Elevation *—Obviously two walls

(b) Plan – Well, perhaps

vertical joint xx

Boundary!

Fig. 30.

closely at the facts, to be the latter. The plans showed both houses built with $4\frac{1}{2}$ inch brick outer skins. They had in fact both been given 6 inch stonework outer skins. The inner skins and the cavities were placed exactly where they were shown on the plan, but that meant that the space between the outer faces had contracted.

Solid objects, such as houses, garages, garden sheds, green-houses, and so on, are not likely to take up their beds and walk. When you find a fence, therefore, erected later than a substantial tool shed, underneath the eaves of the shed, and the eaves were for-merly within the curtilage of the shed's owner, you can safely assume that the fence is trespassing.

Oh no you can't. I was dismayed, having made that assump-tion, to hear the fencing contractor say that he and his gang had shoved the shed aside in order to erect the fence, and had then

79

shoved it back again – just too far. Fortunately, this did not destroy the basis of my evidence (we were in court) though it did move my line a little. How was I to know that the shed could move? Answer: by looking a little more carefully at how solidly it was fixed to the base.

If you are looking at a series of OS maps, ranging over a hundred years or so, and in all of them the corner of the garden of number 49 High Street – or whatever – is in more or less the same position, even though its shape varies a little from year to year, it is only reasonable to assume that it hasn't moved. That obviously then provides you with a fixed point from which other boundaries can start.

Oh no it doesn't. It may do, but unless you have made overlays to ensure that the garden has not been enlarged by purchase from neighbouring landowners (or other means) you can't be sure. It came as a very nasty shock to me when I was asked by counsel, in cross-examination, to lay a 1969 map over a 1938 one. The difference in size of the two gardens, and the movement of the corner upon which I was relying, was too great to be explained away as a variation in free-hand drawing.

As in the last case, it did not destroy my conclusions, but it removed the absolute certainty which I had claimed for one of my starting points.

I was recently telephoned by a lady in Shepherd's Bush who said that her neighbour disagreed that the front fence should be at other than a right angle to the house. 'Stupid woman', I thought. 'Of course it should be at a right angle.' 'What about the deeds?' I asked, out loud. 'Do they show an angle?' 'Oh yes', she said, and I thought: 'The silly woman can't read deeds either.' She insisted that I come to look. So I went.

The deeds showed that not only hers, but the six or so adjoining houses also had boundaries at a funny angle, and the fences showed this on site. Clever woman, Miss Eagle, and we're now very good friends. Clients aren't always wrong, so look at everything with an open mind.

I have warned you elsewhere not to assume that you can rely absolutely upon legal presumptions. I would refer you back to the chapter on 'Garden walls, fences, and bits of string' to review that warning, but I would repeat it here. Indeed, I will go further: never simply assume anything. Check, look, read, think, and then conclude, but always state what assumptions you have been forced to make in order to arrive at your conclusion.

It causes me some distress to observe that this chapter is so long – and I haven't even told you, since I'm not writing about rights of light, about the time when I was completely deceived about the age of a window, so skilfully had it been moved from one position in a wall and matched into another. It is some consolation to be able to use the errors of my youth to warn my successors against following in my erroneous footsteps, but even more to reflect that the last two court cases described, which both occurred quite recently, resulted in complete victory for my clients. Despite the small incorrect assumption which I had made in each case, my general conclusions were upheld and my drawings of the boundary lines were accepted.

Chapter 20

Conclusion

I have said – probably too often already, but that isn't going to stop me saying it yet again – throughout this book, that if I have three words of advice about boundary disputes, they are these:

Don't have them.

If there is a point of doubt, consult before acting. 'Agree with thine adversary quickly, whiles thou art in the way with him', rather than ignore him until he serves a writ. (I expect that some of my colleagues are by now gratified by that other Biblical quotation: 'My desire is ... that mine adversary had written a book.') It is never, never – well, hardly ever – worth going to law (or arbitration) about a small piece of garden; most unlikely to be worth while doing so about part of a field; and seldom, if ever, done about city centre land. A stitch in time of friendly discussion – which is what almost invariably happens in the last sort of case – saves nine poundsworth of fees.

Those remarks are really addressed to the people who own the boundless or disputed land. Now I turn to the surveyors who may be called in to solve the problems.

Don't hesitate to disagree with your client. If you don't think his case carries weight, say so. He will rarely thank you for saving him from vast expenditure, but you will have the satisfaction of knowing that you have done so. As it happens, I am going out to supper this very evening with the only man I have known to thank his surveyor (not me) for turning down a house he wanted to buy, recognising that he was thus being saved from buying a pig in a poke. (He is also the husband of my excellent indexer.)

Use your eyes in every direction. Ask for documents. Ask again. Examine the evidence. Don't limit yourself to the immediate confines of the plot. See if there are nearby comparables that will help. Use the local library for early OS maps. Ask the local newspaper for any relevant photos. Don't jump to conclusions.

Don't be afraid to say that you don't know. Say what you do

know, and express the limitations of what you can only guess at, while indicating how well-founded your assumptions are.

When you are absolutely certain that you have formed a correct view, that your client has understood and agrees with it, and that he fully appreciates how much even successful litigation is likely to cost him, then you should read the chapter on being an expert witness, so as to give your client the best chance of success. Even better than that, however – and I promise that this is the last time you will read it in this book – would be to persuade the neighbours to agree or, failing that, to compromise.

Boundary disputes always profit lawyers; usually profit surveyors; never profit the owners.

Index

Note: **Bold figures indicate major references**